MW00823981

Keto Air Fryer Cookbook with Pictures

Cook and Taste Tens of Low-Carb Fried Recipes. Shed Weight, Kill Hunger, and Regain Confidence Living the Keto Lifestyle

By

Sabrina Malcontenta

This document is geared towards providing exact and reliable information in regards to the topic and issue covered. The publication is sold with the idea that the publisher is not required to render accounting, officially permitted, or otherwise, qualified services. If advice is necessary, legal or professional, a practiced individual in the profession should be ordered.

- From a Declaration of Principles which was accepted and approved equally by a Committee of the American Bar Association and a Committee of Publishers and Associations.

The information provided herein is stated to be truthful and consistent, in that any liability, in terms of inattention or otherwise, by any usage or abuse of any policies, processes, or directions contained within is the solitary and utter responsibility of the recipient reader. Under no circumstances will any legal responsibility or blame be held against the publisher for any reparation, damages, or monetary loss due to the information herein, either directly or indirectly.

Respective authors own all copyrights not held by the publisher.

The information herein is offered for informational purposes solely, and is universal as so. The presentation of the information is without contract or any type of guarantee assurance.

The trademarks that are used are without any consent, and the publication of the trademark is without permission or backing by the trademark owner. All trademarks and brands within this book are for clarifying purposes only and are the owned by the owners themselves, not affiliated with this document.

Contents

Introduction

An air-fryer is a modern kitchen device that cooks food instead of using oil by blowing extremely hot air around it. It provides a low-fat variant of food that in a deep fryer will usually be fried. Consequently, fatty foods such as French fries, fried chicken, and onion rings are usually prepared with no oil or up to 80% less fat relative to traditional cooking techniques.

If you already have an air fryer, you probably know that it's a futuristic gadget designed to save time and help make your life easier. You'll be eager to hear about how soon you'll be addicted to using your air fryer for cooking almost any meal if you've still not taken the jump. What is so unique about air frying, though?

The air fryer will substitute your deep fryer, microwave, oven, and dehydrator and cook tasty meals uniformly in a very small amount of time. Your air fryer is a show stopper if you're trying to help your friends with nutritious food but do not have much time.

With your progress on the ketogenic diet, an air fryer will also aid. The fast cooking time it offers is one of the main advantages of air frying. When you are starving and limited on resources, this is extremely helpful, a formula for cheating on your keto diet. Simple planning of nutritious meals is also linked to long-term progress on a keto diet. That's why during your keto trip, your air fryer can be your best buddy and support you to stay on track, even on days when time is limited for you.

The Air Fryer offers fried foods and nutritious meals, helping you eliminate the calories that come with fried foods and providing you the crunchiness, taste, and flavor you love. By blowing very hot air (up to 400 ° F) uniformly and rapidly around a food ingredient put in an enclosed room, this household appliance works. The heat renders the food part on the outside crispy and brittle, but it is warm and moist on the inside. You can use an air fryer on pretty much everything. You should barbecue, bake and roast in addition to frying. Its choice of cooking choices allows it simpler at any time of the day to eat any food.

Cooking using an Air Fryer

It is as simple to cook with an air fryer as using an oven. Anyone may do it, and then you'll wish that you had turned to this brilliant cooking process earlier after only a few tries. This section will outline air frying choices, optimize your cooking period and juiciness, clarify how to make your air fryer clean and offer some gadgets that will make sure that your air frying experience is even simpler and more pleasant.

Although the fundamentals of using an air fryer would be discussed in this section, the first phase is studying the guide that comes along with the air fryer. Almost all air fryers are distinct, and there are several different versions of the industry with the recent spike in device demand. Knowing how to thoroughly operate your particular air fryer is the secret to victory and can familiarize you with debugging concerns as well as protection features. Until first use, reading through the guide and washing every component with soft, soapy water can make you feel prepared to release your cooking finesse!

Why Use It:

Air frying is widely common because it enables you to cook tasty meals easily and uniformly with very small quantity of oil and very little energy. Here are only a handful of reasons to turn to air frying:

Quick cleanup: You would certainly stain your cooker with every cooking process, but with the smaller frying region of the air fryer and portable basket, comprehensive cleanup is a breeze!

Cooks faster: By rotating heated air throughout the cooking compartment, air frying operates. This contributes to quick and even frying, using a portion of your oven's resources. You can set most air fryers to an extreme temperature of around 350-400°F. Because of which, in an air fryer, you can cook just about everything you can create in a microwave.

Low-Fat Food: The most important feature of the air fryer is the usage of hot-air airflow to cook food products from all directions, removing the need for gasoline. This makes it easier for individuals on a reduced-fat diet to eat deliciously balanced meals safely.

Highly Safe: While tossing chicken or any other ingredients into the deep fryer, do you know how extra cautious you have to be? As it is still really hot, you want to be sure that the hot oil does not spill and damage your face. You wouldn't have to think about brunette skin from hot oil spillage with your air fryer.

Multifunctional Use: Since it can cook many dishes at once, the air fryer helps you multitask. It is your all-in-one gadget that can barbecue, bake, fry and roast the dishes you need! For separate work, you no longer require several appliances.

Healthier Foods: Air fryers are built to operate without fattening oils and up to 80 percent less fat to create healthier foods. This makes it possible to lose weight because you can also enjoy your fried dishes while retaining calories and saturated fat. Through utilizing this appliance, making the transition to a healthy existence is more feasible. The scent that comes with deep-fried items, which also hangs in the room even many hours after deep frying, is also eliminated from your house.

Selecting a Custom Air Fryer:

The dual most significant aspects to concentrate on are scale/size and heat range when picking an air fryer. In general, quart scale air fryers are calculated and vary from around 1.2 quarts size to about 10 quarts or even more. You may be drawn in at a minimum a 5.3-quart fryer which may be used to wonderfully roast a whole chicken if you are trying to prepare meals to serve a group, but if you require a tiny machine owing to the minimal counter room and you are preparing for just one or two, you can certainly crisp up those Fries with a much minor air fryer.

And for the range of temperatures available, many air fryers encourage you to dry out foods and, for a prolonged period, you can fry them at extremely low heat, say about 120 ° F. You'll want to ensure the air fryer takes the necessary cooking power and heat range, based on the functions you use.

Accessories

The cooking chamber of your air fryer is essentially just a wide, open room for the warm air to move. It is a big bonus because it offers you the opportunity to integrate into your kitchen some different accessories. These devices increase the amount of dishes that you can produce using your air fryer and start opening choices that you might never have known was feasible. Below are few of the popular gadgets.

Parchment: In specific, precut parchment may be useful while baking with your air fryer to make cleaning much simpler. Similarly, for quick steaming, you will find parchment paper with precut holes.

Pizza pan: Indeed, using the air fryer, you can make a pizza, and this book contains many recipes for various kinds of keto-friendly pizzas. This is a fantastic alternative to still have the desired form quickly.

Cupcake pan: It typically comes with several tiny cups, and the 5.3-quart size air fryer takes up the whole chamber. For cupcakes, muffins, or even egg plates, these flexible cups are fine. You can still use single silicone baking containers if you would not want to go this path.

Cake pan: For your air fryer, you will find specially designed cake pans that fit perfectly into the inner pot. They even come with a built-in handle so that when your cakes are finished baking, you can quickly take them out.

Skewer rack: This is identical to a holder made of aluminum, except it has built-in skewers of metal that make roasting kebabs a breeze.

Metal holder: To add a layer to your cooking plate, this round rack is used so that you can optimize room and cook several items simultaneously. When you cook meat and vegetables and don't want to stop to cook to get going on the other, this is especially helpful.

How to clean an Air Fryer

Make sure that the air fryer is cold and unhooked before washing it. To wash the air fryer slate, you'll need to follow the steps below:

1. Separate your air fryer plate from its foundation. Fill a tub of worm water and soap for your pan. Let the plate sit in warm water and soap mix for about 10 minutes with your frying bucket inside.
2. Using a brush or sponge, thoroughly clean the bucket.
3. Lift the basket from the frying pan and clean the underneath and exterior surfaces.
4. Now use the same brush or sponge to clean your air-fryer plate.
5. Allow all to air-dry completely and transfer to the foundation of the air fryer.

Simply scrub the exterior with a wet cloth to disinfect the exterior of your air fryer. Then, before starting your next cooking experience, make sure all parts are in there right places.

Keto Diet

A relatively moderate-protein, low-carb, and elevated diet that help the body sustain itself without using sugars or high amounts of carbs is the keto diet or keto. When the system is low on glucose (sugar), ketones are formed by a mechanism called ketosis in the liver from food metabolism. This diet will contribute to some lower blood sugar, weight loss, balanced insulin levels, plus managed cravings, with diligent monitoring, imaginative meals, and self-control.

Your body takes some carbohydrates as you consume high-carb nutrition and converts them into energy to fuel itself. Your liver instead burns fat as you leave out the carbohydrates. A ketogenic régime usually limits carbohydrates to about 0-50 grams a day.

Tips for Usage:
- Preheat your fryer before use
- Always cook in batches. Do not overcrowd your fryer
- Space Your Foods evenly when added to the air fryer
- Keep It Dry
- Use spray oil to oil your food

CHAPTER 1: Breakfast Recipes

If you set your air fryer to work, simple and healthy low-carb breakfasts will soon be the rule in your home! These meals will boot the day in a nutritious way without robbing you of days that should be full of savory fun! It can be not easy to make a nourishing meal for oneself or relatives while you're trying to get out of the house in time. The easiest choice might be to catch a granola bar or microwave pastry, but it will quickly contribute to thoughts of shame and guilt and extreme malnutrition at noon.

This section's meals are full and keto-approved, making you improve your mornings and all your days. Get prepared in a snap for nutritious meals that can be created using your air fryer. You can make meals in advance, such as Cheese Balls, and Sausage and you can put dishes in the air fryer to get ready until you get dressed, such as Quick and Simple Bacon Strips, you'll want to have begun frying your breakfasts earlier!

1. Loaded Cauliflower Breakfast Bake

Preparation time: 15 minutes

Cooking time: 20 minutes

Servings: 4 people

Ingredients:

- 12 slices sugar-free bacon, cooked and crumbled
- 2 scallions, sliced on the bias
- 8 tablespoons full-fat sour cream
- 1 medium avocado, peeled and pitted
- 1 cup shredded medium Cheddar cheese
- 11/2 cups chopped cauliflower
- 1/4 cup heavy whipping cream
- 6 large eggs

Directions:

1. Mix the eggs and milk in a medium dish. Pour it into a circular 4-cup baking tray.

2. Add and blend the cauliflower, and cover it with cheddar. Put your dish in the air-fryer bowl.

3. Change the temperature and set the timer to about 320°F for around 20 minutes.

4. The eggs will be solid once fully baked, and the cheese will be golden brown. Slice it into 4 bits.

5. Cut the avocado and split the bits equally. Put two teaspoons of sliced scallions, sour cream, and crumbled bacon on top of each plate.

2. Scrambled Eggs

Preparation time: 5 minutes

Cooking time: 20 minutes

Servings: 2 people

Ingredients:

- 1/2 cup shredded sharp Cheddar cheese
- 2 tablespoons unsalted butter, melted
- 4 large eggs

Directions:

1. Crack the eggs into a round 2-cup baking pan and whisk them. Put the tray in the air-fryer container.

2. Change the temperature settings and set the timer to about 400°F for around 10 minutes.

3. Mix the eggs after about 5 minutes and add some cheese and butter. Let it cook for another 3 minutes and mix again.

4. Give an extra 2 minutes to finish frying or remove the eggs from flame if they are to your preferred taste.

5. For fluffing, use a fork. Serve it hot.

3. "Hard-Boiled" Eggs

Preparation time: 2 minutes

Cooking time: 20 minutes

Servings: 4 people

Ingredients:

- 1 cup water
- 4 large eggs

Directions:

1. Put the eggs in a heat-proof 4-cup round baking tray and pour some water over your eggs. Put the tray in the air-fryer basket.

2. Set the air fryer's temperature to about 300 ° F and set the clock for about 18-minute.

3. In the fridge, store boiled eggs before ready to consume or peel and serve warmly.

4. Breakfast Stuffed Poblanos

Preparation time: 20 minutes

Cooking time: 15 minutes

Servings: 5 people

Ingredients:

- 1/2 cup full-fat sour cream
- 8 tablespoons shredded pepper jack cheese
- 4 large poblano peppers
- 1/4 cup canned diced tomatoes and green chilies, drained
- 4 ounces full-fat cream cheese, softened
- 4 large eggs
- 1/2 pound spicy ground pork breakfast sausage

Directions:

1. Crumble and brown the cooked sausage in a large skillet over medium-low heat until no red exists. Take the sausage from the skillet and clean the oil. Crack your eggs in the skillet, scramble, and simmer until they are no longer watery.

2. In a wide bowl, add the fried sausage and add in cream cheese. Mix the sliced tomatoes and chilies. Gently fold the eggs together.

3. Cut a 4-5-inch gap at the top of each poblano, separating the white layer and seeds with a tiny knife. In four

portions, divide the filling and gently scoop into each pepper. Cover each with 2 teaspoons of cheese from the pepper jack.

4. Drop each pepper into the container of the air fryer.

5. Change the temperature and set the timer to about 350 °F for around 15 minutes.

6. The peppers will be tender, and when prepared, the cheese will be golden brown. Serve instantly with sour cream on top.

5. Cheesy Cauliflower Hash Browns

Preparation time: 20 minutes

Cooking time: 12 minutes

Servings: 4 people

Ingredients:

- 1 cup shredded sharp Cheddar cheese
- 1 large egg
- 1 (12-ounce) steamer bag cauliflower

Directions:

1. Put the bag in the oven and cook as per the directions in the box. To extract excess moisture, leave to cool fully and place cauliflower in a cheesecloth or paper towel and squeeze.

2. Add the cheese and eggs and mash the cauliflower using a fork.

3. Cut a slice of parchment to match the frame of your air fryer. Take 1/4 of the paste and make it into a hash-brown patty shape and mold it. Put it on the parchment and, into your air fryer basket, if required, running in groups.

4. Change the temperature and set the clock to about 400°F for around 12 minutes.

5. Halfway into the cooking process, turn your hash browns. They will be nicely browned when fully baked. Instantly serve.

6. Egg, Cheese, and Bacon Roll-Ups

Preparation time: 20 minutes

Cooking time: 20 minutes

Servings: 4 people

Ingredients:

- 1/2 cup mild salsa for dipping
- 1 cup shredded sharp Cheddar cheese
- 12 slices sugar free bacon
- 6 large eggs
- 1/2 medium green bell pepper, seeded and chopped
- 1/4 cup chopped onion
- 2 tablespoons unsalted butter

Directions:

1. Melt the butter in a small skillet over medium flame. Add the pepper and onion to the skillet and sauté until aromatic, around 3 minutes, and your onions are transparent.

2. In a shallow pot, whisk the eggs and dump them into a skillet. Scramble the pepper and onion with the eggs once fluffy and fully fried after 5 minutes. Remove from the flame and set aside.

3. Put 3 strips of bacon beside each other on the cutting board, overlapping about 1/4. Place 1/4 cup of scrambled eggs on the side nearest to you in a pile and scatter 1/4 cup of cheese on top of your eggs.

4. Wrap the bacon around the eggs securely and, if needed, protect the seam using a toothpick. Put each wrap into the container of the air fryer.

5. Switch the temperature to about 350 ° F and set the clock for around 15 minutes. Midway through the cooking time, turn the rolls.

6. When fully fried, the bacon would be brown and tender. For frying, serve immediately with some salsa.

7. Pancake

Preparation time: 10 minutes

Cooking time: 7 minutes

Servings: 4 people

Ingredients:

- 1/2 teaspoon ground cinnamon
- 1/2 teaspoon vanilla extract
- 1/2 teaspoon unflavored gelatin
- 1 large egg
- 2 tablespoons unsalted butter, softened
- 1/2 teaspoon baking powder
- 1/4 cup powdered erythritol
- 1/2 cup blanched finely ground almond flour

Directions:

1. Combine the erythritol, almond flour, and baking powder in a wide pot. Add some egg, butter, cinnamon, gelatin, and vanilla. Place into a rectangular 6-inch baking tray.

2. Place the tray in the container of your air fryer.

3. Change the temperature to about 300 °F and set the clock for 7 minutes.

4. A toothpick can pop out dry when the dessert is fully baked. Split the cake into four servings and eat.

8. Lemon Poppy Seed Cake

Preparation time: 10 minutes

Cooking time: 14 minutes

Servings: 6 people

Ingredients:

- 1 teaspoon poppy seeds
- 1 medium lemon
- 1 teaspoon vanilla extract
- 2 large eggs
- 1/4 cup unsweetened almond milk
- 1/4 cup unsalted butter, melted
- 1/2 teaspoon baking powder
- 1/2 cup powdered erythritol
- 1 cup blanched finely ground almond flour

Directions:

Mix the erythritol, almond flour, butter, baking powder, eggs, almond milk, and vanilla in a big bowl.

Halve the lime and strain the liquid into a little pot, then transfer it to the mixture.

Zest the lemon with a fine grinder and transfer 1 tbsp. of zest to the mixture and blend. Add the poppy seeds to your batter.

In the non-stick 6' circular cake tin, add your batter. Put the pan in the container of your air fryer.

Change the temperature and set the clock to about 300°F for around 14 minutes.

A wooden skewer inserted in the middle, if it comes out completely clean, means it's thoroughly fried. The cake will stop cooking and crisp up when it cools. At room temperature, serve.

9. "Banana" Nut Cake

Preparation time: 20 minutes

Cooking time: 30 minutes

Servings: 6-7 people

Ingredients:

- 1/4 cup of chopped walnuts
- 2 large eggs
- 1/4 cup of full-fat sour cream
- 1 teaspoon of vanilla extract
- 21/2 teaspoons of banana extract
- 1/4 cup of unsalted butter, melted
- 1/2 teaspoon of ground cinnamon
- 2 teaspoons of baking powder
- 2 tablespoons of ground golden flaxseed

- 1/2 cup of powdered erythritol
- 1 cup of blanched finely ground almond flour

Directions:

1. Mix the erythritol, almond flour, baking powder, flaxseed, and cinnamon in a big dish.

2. Add vanilla extract, banana extract, butter, and sour cream and mix well.

3. Add your eggs to the combination and whisk until they are fully mixed. Mix in your walnuts.

4. Pour into a 6-inch non-stick cake pan and put in the bowl of your air fryer.

5. Change the temperature and set the clock to about 300°F for around 25 minutes.

6. When fully baked, the cake will be lightly golden, and a toothpick inserted in the middle will come out clean. To prevent cracking, allow it to cool entirely.

10. Bacon Strips

Preparation time: 5 minutes

Cooking time: 12 minutes

Servings: 5 people

Ingredients:

- 10 slices sugar free bacon

Directions:

1. Put slices of bacon into the bucket of your air fryer.

2. Change the temperature and set the timer to about 400°F for around 12 minutes.

3. Turn the bacon after 6 minutes and proceed to cook. Serve hot.

11. Pumpkin Spice Muffins

Preparation time: 10 minutes

Cooking time: 15 minutes

Servings: 6 people

Ingredients:

- 2 large eggs
- 1 teaspoon vanilla extract
- 1/4 teaspoon ground nutmeg
- 1/2 teaspoon ground cinnamon
- 1/4 cup pure pumpkin purée
- 1/4 cup unsalted butter, softened
- 1/2 teaspoon baking powder
- 1/2 cup granular erythritol
- 1 cup blanched finely ground almond flour

Directions:

1. Mix the erythritol, almond flour, butter, baking powder, nutmeg, cinnamon, pumpkin purée, and vanilla in a big dish.
2. Stir in the eggs softly.
3. Add the batter into about six or more silicone muffin cups equally. Put muffin cups in the air fryer basket. If required, make them in groups.
4. Change the temperature and set the clock to about 300°F for around 15 minutes.
5. A wooden skewer inserted in the middle will come out completely clean if thoroughly cooked. Serve hot.

12. Veggie Frittata

Preparation time: minutes

Cooking time: minutes

Servings: people

Ingredients:

- 1/4 cup of chopped green bell pepper
- 1/4 cup of chopped yellow onion
- 1/2 cup of chopped broccoli
- 1/4 cup of heavy whipping cream
- 6 large eggs

Directions:

1. Whisk the heavy whipping cream and eggs in a big bowl. Add in the onion, broccoli, and bell pepper.

2. Load into a 6-inch circular baking dish that is oven-safe. Put the baking tray in the basket of an air fryer.

3. Switch the temperature to about 350 ° F and set the clock for around 12-minute.

4. When the frittata is finished, eggs must be solid and thoroughly cooked. Serve it hot.

13. Buffalo Egg Cups

Preparation time: 12 minutes

Cooking time: 12 minutes

Servings: 3 people

Ingredients:

- 1/2 cup of shredded sharp Cheddar cheese
- 2 tablespoons of buffalo sauce
- 2 ounces of full-fat cream cheese

- 4 large eggs

Directions:

1. In two (4') ramekins, add the eggs.

2. Mix the buffalo sauce, cream cheese, and cheddar in a little, microwave-safe container. For about 20 seconds, microwave and then mix. Put a spoonful on top of each egg within each ramekin.

3. Put the ramekins in the container of an air fryer.

4. Change the temperature and set the timer to about 320°F for around 15 minutes.

5. Serve it hot.

14. Crispy Southwestern Ham Egg Cups

Preparation time: 5 minutes

Cooking time: 14 minutes

Servings: 3 people

Ingredients:

- 1/2 cup of shredded medium Cheddar cheese
- 2 tablespoons of diced white onion
- 2 tablespoons of diced red bell pepper
- 1/4 cup diced of green bell pepper
- 2 tablespoons of full-fat sour cream
- 4 large eggs
- 4 (1-ounce) of slices deli ham

Directions:

1. Put a piece of ham at the bottom of four or more baking cups.

2. Whisk the eggs along with the sour cream in a big bowl. Add the red pepper, green pepper, and onion and mix well.

3. Add the mixture of eggs into baking cups that are ham-lined. Top them with some cheddar cheese. Put the cups in the container of your air fryer.

4. Set the clock for around 12 minutes or till the peaks are golden browned, cook at a temperature of about 320 ° F.

5. Serve it hot.

15. Jalapeño Popper Egg Cups

Preparation time: 10 minutes

Cooking time: 12 minutes

Servings: 3 people

Ingredients:

- 1/2 cup of shredded sharp Cheddar cheese
- 2 ounces of full-fat cream cheese
- 1/4 cup of chopped pickled jalapeños
- 4 large eggs

Directions:

1. Add the eggs to a medium container, and then dump them into 4 silicone muffin cups.

2. Place the cream cheese, jalapeños, and cheddar in a wide, microwave-safe dish. Heat in the microwave for about 30 seconds and mix well. Take a full spoon and put it in the middle of one of the egg cups, around 1/4 of the paste. Repeat for the mixture left.

3. Put the egg cups in the container of your air fryer.

4. Change the temperature and set the clock for around 10 minutes to about 320 °F.

5. Serve it hot.

16. Crunchy Granola

Preparation time: 10 minutes

Cooking time: 5 minutes

Servings: 6 people

Ingredients:

- 1 teaspoon of ground cinnamon
- 2 tablespoons of unsalted butter
- 1/4 cup of granular erythritol
- 1/4 cup of low-carb, sugar free chocolate chips
- 1/4 cup of golden flaxseed
- 1/3 cup of sunflower seeds
- 1 cup of almond slivers
- 1 cup of unsweetened coconut flakes
- 2 cups of pecans, chopped

Directions:

1. Blend all the ingredients in a big bowl.

2. In a 4-cup circular baking tray, put the mixture into it.

3. Place the tray in the air-fryer container.

4. Change the temperature and set the clock to about 320°F for around 5 minutes.

5. Let it cool absolutely before serving.

CHAPTER 2: Air Fryer Chicken Main Dishes

1. Chicken Fajitas

Preparation time: 10 minutes

Cooking time: 15 minutes

Servings: 2 people

Ingredients:

- 1/2 medium red bell pepper, seeded and sliced
- 1/2 medium green bell pepper, seeded and sliced
- 1/4 medium onion, peeled and sliced
- 1/2 teaspoon garlic powder
- 1/2 teaspoon paprika
- 1/2 teaspoon cumin
- 1 tablespoon chili powder
- 2 tablespoons coconut oil, melted
- 10 ounces boneless, skinless chicken breast, sliced into 1/4" strips

Directions:

1. In a big bowl, mix the chicken and coconut oil and scatter with the paprika, cumin, chili powder, and garlic powder. Toss the chicken with spices until well mixed. Put the chicken in the basket of an air fryer.

2. Set the temperature and adjust the clock to about 350°F for around 15 minutes.

3. When your clock has 7 minutes left, throw in the peppers and onion into the fryer bucket.

4. When frying, flip the chicken at least two to three times. Veggies should be soft; when done, the chicken should be thoroughly cooked to at least 165°F internal temperature. Serve it hot.

2. Pepperoni and Chicken Pizza Bake

Preparation time: 10 minutes

Cooking time: 15 minutes

Servings: 4 people

Ingredients:

- 1/4 cup grated Parmesan cheese
- 1 cup shredded mozzarella cheese
- 1 cup low-carb, sugar-free pizza sauce
- 20 slices pepperoni
- 2 cups cubed cooked chicken

Directions:

1. Add the pepperoni, chicken, and pizza sauce into a 4-cup rectangular baking tray. Stir such that the beef is coated fully in the sauce.

2. Cover with grated mozzarella and parmesan. Put your dish in the air-fryer bucket.

3. Set the temperature and adjust the clock to about 375°F for around 15 minutes.

4. When served, the dish would be brown and bubbly. Instantly serve.

3. Almond-Crusted Chicken

Preparation time: 15 minutes

Cooking time: 25 minutes

Servings: 4 people

Ingredients:

- 1 tablespoon Dijon mustard
- 2 tablespoons full-fat mayonnaise
- 2 (6-ounce) boneless, skinless chicken breasts
- 1/4 cup slivered almonds

Directions:

1. In a food processor, pulse your almonds or cut until finely diced. Put the almonds equally and put them aside on a tray.
2. Completely split each chicken breast lengthwise in part.
3. In a shallow pot, combine the mustard and mayonnaise now, cover the entire chicken with the mixture.
4. Place each piece of chicken completely coated in the diced almonds. Transfer the chicken gently into the bucket of your air fryer.
5. Set the temperature and adjust the clock to about 350°F for around 25 minutes.

6. When it has hit an interior temperature of about 165 ° F or more, the chicken will be cooked. Serve it hot.

4. Southern "Fried" Chicken

Preparation time: 15 minutes

Cooking time: 25 minutes

Servings: 4 people

Ingredients:

- 2 ounces pork rinds, finely ground

- 1/4 teaspoon ground black pepper

- 1/4 teaspoon onion powder

- 1/2 teaspoon cumin

- 1 tablespoon chili powder

- 2 tablespoons hot sauce

- 2 (6-ounce) boneless, skinless chicken breasts

Directions:

1. Longitudinally, split each chicken breast in half. Put the chicken in a big pot and add some hot sauce to coat the chicken completely.

2. Mix the onion powder, cumin, chili powder, and pepper in a shallow container. Sprinkle the mix over your chicken.

3. In a wide bowl, put the seasoned pork rinds and dunk each chicken piece into the container, covering as much as necessary. Put the chicken in the bucket of an air fryer.

4. Set the temperature and adjust the clock to about 350°F for around 25 minutes.

5. Turn the chicken gently midway through the cooking process.

6. The internal temperature will be at most 165 ° F when finished, and the coating of the pork rind will be rich golden brown in color. Serve it hot.

5. Spinach and Feta-Stuffed Chicken Breast

Preparation time: 15 minutes

Cooking time: 25 minutes

Servings: 2 people

Ingredients:

- 1 tablespoon coconut oil
- 2 (6-ounce) boneless, skinless chicken breasts
- 1/4 cup crumbled feta

- 1/4 cup chopped yellow onion
- 1/2 teaspoon salt, divided
- 1/2 teaspoon garlic powder, divided
- 5 ounces frozen spinach, thawed and drained
- 1 tablespoon unsalted butter

Directions:

1. Add some butter to your pan and sauté the spinach for around 3 minutes in a medium-sized skillet over a medium-high flame. Sprinkle the spinach with 1/4 teaspoon salt, 1/4 teaspoon garlic powder now, add your onion to the plate.

2. Sauté for another 3 minutes, then turn off the flame and put it in a medium-sized dish. Fold the feta mixture into the spinach.

3. Lengthwise, carve a nearly 4' cut through the side of each chicken breast. Scoop half of the mix into each portion and seal with a pair of toothpicks shut. Dust with leftover salt and garlic powder outside of your chicken. Drizzle some coconut oil. Put the chicken breasts in the bucket of your air fryer.

4. Set the temperature and adjust the clock to about 350°F for around 25 minutes.

5. The chicken must be golden brown in color and have an internal temperature of at least 165 ° F when fully cooked. Cut and serve hot.

6. Blackened Cajun Chicken Tenders

Preparation time: 10 minutes

Cooking time: 17 minutes

Servings: 4 people

Ingredients:

- 1/4 cup full-fat ranch dressing
- 1 pound boneless, skinless chicken tenders
- 2 tablespoons coconut oil
- 1/8 teaspoon ground cayenne pepper
- 1/4 teaspoon onion powder
- 1/2 teaspoon dried thyme
- 1/2 teaspoon garlic powder
- 1 teaspoon chili powder
- 2 teaspoons paprika

Directions:

1. Mix all the seasonings in a shallow container.
2. Drizzle oil over chicken wings and then cover each tender thoroughly in the mixture of spices. Put tenders in the bucket of your air fryer.
3. Set the temperature and adjust the clock to about 375 °F for around 17 minutes.

4. Tenders, when completely baked, will have a temperature of 165 ° F centrally.

5. For dipping, use some ranch dressing and enjoy.

7. Chicken Pizza Crust

Preparation time: 10 minutes

Cooking time: 25 minutes

Servings: 4 people

Ingredients:

1 pound ground chicken thigh meat

1/4 cup grated Parmesan cheese

1/2 cup shredded mozzarella

Directions:

1. Combine all the ingredients in a wide bowl. Split equally into four portions.

2. Slice out four (6") parchment paper circles and push down the chicken mixture on each one of the circles. Put into the bucket of your air fryer, working as required in groups or individually.

3. Set the temperature and adjust the clock to about 375°F for around 25 minutes.

4. Midway into the cooking process, turn the crust.

5. You can cover it with some cheese and your choice of toppings until completely baked, and cook for 5 extra

minutes. Or, you can place the crust in the fridge or freezer and top it later when you are ready to consume.

8. Chicken Enchiladas

Preparation time: 20 minutes

Cooking time: 10 minutes

Servings: 4 people

Ingredients:

- 1 medium avocado, peeled, pitted, and sliced
- Half cup full-fat sour cream
- 1 cup shredded medium Cheddar cheese
- Half cup of torn Monterey jack (MJ) cheese
- 1/2 pound medium-sliced deli chicken
- 1/3 cup low-carb enchilada sauce, divided
- 1 1/2 cups shredded cooked chicken

Directions:

1. Combine the shredded chicken and at least half of the enchilada sauce in a big dish. On a cutting surface, lay pieces of deli chicken and pour 2 teaspoons of shredded chicken mixture on each of your slices.

2. Sprinkle each roll with 2 teaspoons of cheddar cheese. Roll softly to close it completely.

3. Put each roll, seam side down, in a 4-cup circular baking tray. Over the rolls, pour the leftover sauce and top with the Monterey Jack. Put the dish in the air-fryer basket.

4. Set the temperature and adjust the clock to about 370 °F for around 10 minutes.

5. Enchiladas, when baked, would be golden on top and bubbling. With some sour cream and diced avocado, serve hot.

9. Jalapeño Popper Hassel back Chicken

Preparation time: 20 minutes

Cooking time: 20 minutes

Servings: 4 people

Ingredients:

- 2 (6-ounce) boneless, skinless chicken breasts
- 1/4 cup sliced pickled jalapeños
- 1/2 cup shredded sharp Cheddar cheese, divided
- 2 ounces full-fat cream cheese, softened
- 4 slices sugar-free bacon, cooked and crumbled

Directions:

1. Put the fried bacon in a medium-sized dish; add in half of the cheddar, cream cheese, and the jalapeño strips.

1. Using a sharp knife to build slits around 3/4 of the way across the chicken in each of the chicken thighs, being cautious not to go all the way through. You would typically get 6 to 8 per breast, cuts based on the chicken breast's length.

2. Spoon the premade cream cheese mix onto the chicken strips. Toss the leftover shredded cheese over your chicken breasts and put it in the air fryer basket.

3. Set the temperature and adjust the clock to about 350°F for around 20 minutes.

4. Serve it hot.

10. Chicken Cordon Bleu Casserole

Preparation time: 15 minutes

Cooking time: 15 minutes

Servings: 4 people

Ingredients:

- 1-ounce pork rinds, crushed
- 2 teaspoons Dijon mustard
- 2 tablespoons unsalted butter, melted
- 1 tablespoon heavy cream
- 4 ounces full-fat cream cheese, softened
- 2 ounces Swiss cheese, cubed

- 1/2 cup cubed cooked ham
- 2 cups cubed cooked chicken thigh meat

Directions:

1. Put the chicken and ham in a 6-inch circular baking pan and toss to blend the meat uniformly. Scatter on top of the meat some cheese cubes.

2. Add butter, heavy cream, cream cheese, and mustard in a big bowl and then spill the mix over your meat and cheese. Cover with rinds of pork. Put the pan in the bucket of your air fryer.

3. Set the temperature and adjust the clock to about 350°F for around 15 minutes.

4. When finished, the saucepan will be caramelized and bubbling. Serve hot.

11. Chicken Parmesan

Preparation time: 10 minutes

Cooking time: 25 minutes

Servings: 4 people

Ingredients:

- 1-ounce pork rinds, crushed
- 1 cup low-carb, no-sugar-added pasta sauce
- 1/2 cup grated Parmesan cheese, divided
- 2 (6-ounce) boneless, skinless chicken breasts
- 1 cup shredded mozzarella cheese, divided

- 4 tablespoons full-fat mayonnaise, divided
- 1/2 teaspoon dried parsley
- 1/4 teaspoon dried oregano
- 1/2 teaspoon garlic powder

Directions:

1. Cut each chicken breast longitudinally in half and hammer it to pound out a thickness of about 3/4". Sprinkle with parsley, garlic powder, and oregano.

2. On top of each slice of chicken, scatter 1 tablespoon of mayonnaise, then cover each piece with 1/4 cup of mozzarella.

3. Mix the shredded parmesan and pork rinds in a shallow bowl. Sprinkle the surface of the mozzarella with the paste.

4. In a 6' circular baking tray, transfer the sauce and put the chicken on top. Place the pan in the bucket of your air fryer.

5. Set the temperature and adjust the clock to about 320 ° F for around 25 minutes.

6. The cheese will be light browned, and when completely baked, the chicken's internal temperature will be at about 165 ° F. Serve hot.

12. Fajita-Stuffed Chicken Breast

Preparation time: 15 minutes

Cooking time: 25 minutes

Servings: 4 people

Ingredients:

- 1/2 teaspoon garlic powder
- 1 teaspoon ground cumin
- 2 teaspoons chili powder
- 1 tablespoon coconut oil
- 1 medium green bell pepper, seeded and sliced
- 1/4 medium white onion, peeled and sliced
- 2 (6-ounce) boneless, skinless chicken breasts

Directions:

1. "Slice each chicken breast into two equal parts entirely in half longitudinally. Hammer the chicken out until it is around 1/4" thick using a meat mallet.

2. Put out each chicken slice and arrange three onion pieces and four green pepper pieces on end nearest to you. Start to firmly roll the onions and peppers into the chicken. Both with toothpicks or a few strips of butcher's twine protect the roll.

3. Drizzle the chicken with coconut oil. Sprinkle with cumin, chili powder, and garlic powder on either side. Put all the rolls in the bucket of your air fryer.

4. Set the temperature and adjust the clock to about 350°F for around 25 minutes.

5. Serve it hot.

13. Lemon Pepper Drumsticks

Preparation time: 5 minutes

Cooking time: 22 minutes

Servings: 4 people

Ingredients:

- 1 tablespoon lemon pepper seasoning
- 4 tablespoons salted butter, melted
- 8 chicken drumsticks
- 1/2 teaspoon garlic powder
- 2 teaspoons baking powder

Directions:

1. Sprinkle some baking powder over the drumsticks along with some garlic powder and massage it into the chicken skin. Add your drumsticks into the bucket of your air fryer.

2. Set the temperature and adjust the clock to about 375°F for around 25 minutes.

3. Turn your drumsticks midway through the cooking process using tongs.

4. Take out from the fryer when the skin is golden in color, and the inside temperature is at a minimum of 165 ° F.

5. Put lemon pepper seasoning and some butter in a big dish. To the dish, add your fried drumsticks and turn until the chicken is coated. Serve it hot.

14. Cilantro Lime Chicken Thighs

Preparation time: 15 minutes

Cooking time: 22 minutes

Servings: 4 people

Ingredients:

- 1/4 cup chopped fresh cilantro
- 2 medium limes
- 1 teaspoon cumin
- 2 teaspoons chili powder
- 1/2 teaspoon garlic powder
- 1 teaspoon baking powder
- 4 bone-in, skin-on chicken thighs

Directions:

1. Toss some baking powder on your chicken thighs and rinse them.

2. Mix the chili powder, garlic powder, and cumin in a small bowl and sprinkle uniformly over the thighs, rubbing softly on and under the chicken's skin.

3. Halve one lime and squeeze the liquid across the thighs. Place the chicken in the bucket of an air fryer.

4. Set the temperature and adjust the clock to about 380°F for around 22-minute.

5. For serving, split the other lime into four slices and garnish the fried chicken with lemon wedges and some cilantro.

15. Lemon Thyme Roasted Chicken

Preparation time: 10 minutes

Cooking time: 60 minutes

Servings: 6 people

Ingredients:

- 2 tablespoons salted butter, melted
- 1 medium lemon
- 1 teaspoon baking powder
- 1/2 teaspoon onion powder 2 teaspoons dried parsley
- 1 teaspoon garlic powder
- 2 teaspoons dried thyme
- 1 (4-pound) chicken

Directions:

1. Rub the garlic powder, thyme, parsley, onion powder, and baking powder with the chicken.

2. Slice the lemon put four slices using a toothpick on top of the chicken, chest side up, and secure. Put the leftover slices inside your chicken.

3. Put the whole chicken in the bucket of your air fryer, chest side down.

4. Set the temperature and adjust the clock to about 350°F for around 60-minute.

5. Switch the sides of your chicken after 30 minutes, so its breast side is up.

6. The internal temperature should be at about 165 ° F when finished, and the skin should be golden in color and crispy. Pour the melted butter over the whole chicken before serving.

16. Teriyaki Wings

Preparation time: 60 minutes

Cooking time: 45 minutes

Servings: 4 people

Ingredients:

- 2 teaspoons baking powder
- 1/4 teaspoon ground ginger
- 2 teaspoons minced garlic

- 1/2 cup sugar-free teriyaki sauce
- 2 pounds chicken wings

Directions:

1. Put all of your ingredients in a big bowl or bag, excluding the baking powder and leave to marinate in the fridge for at least 1 hour.

2. Bring the wings into the bucket of your air fryer and dust with baking powder. Rub the wings softly.

3. Set the temperature and adjust the clock to about 400°F for around 25 minutes.

4. When frying, rotate the bucket two to three times.

5. Wings, when finished, should be crunchy and cooked internally to a minimum 165 ° F. Instantly serve.

17. Crispy Buffalo Chicken Tenders

Preparation time: 15 minutes

Cooking time: 20 minutes

Servings: 4 people

Ingredients:

- 1 teaspoon garlic powder
- 1 teaspoon chili powder
- 11/2 ounces pork rinds, finely ground
- 1/4 cup hot sauce
- 1 pound boneless, skinless chicken tenders

Directions:

1. Put the chicken tenders in a big bowl and pour them over with hot sauce. In the hot sauce, toss tender, rubbing uniformly.

2. Mix the ground pork rinds with chili powder and garlic powder in a separate, wide bowl.

3. Put each tender, fully coated, in the ground pork rinds. With some water, wet your hands and push down the rinds of pork onto the chicken.

4. Put the tenders in a single layer into the basket of the air fryer.

5. Set the temperature and adjust the clock to about 375°F for around 20 minutes.

6. Serve it hot.

CHAPTER 3: Air Fryer Side Dish Recipes

1. Pita-Style Chips

Preparation time: 10 minutes

Cooking time: 5 minutes

Servings: 4 people

Ingredients:

- 1 large egg
- 1/4 cup blanched finely ground almond flour
- 1/2 ounce pork rinds, finely ground
- 1 cup shredded mozzarella cheese

Directions:

1. Put mozzarella in a wide oven-safe dish and microwave for about 30 seconds or until melted. Add the rest of the ingredients and mix until largely smooth dough shapes into a ball quickly; if your dough is too hard, microwave for an additional 15 seconds.

2. Roll the dough into a wide rectangle among two parchment paper sheets and then use a sharp knife to make the triangle-shaped chips. Put the prepared chips in the bucket of your air fryer.

3. Set the temperature and adjust the clock to about 350°F for around 5 minutes.

4. Chips, when finished, would be golden in color and crunchy. When they cool down, they will become even crispier.

2. Avocado Fries

Preparation time: 15 minutes

Cooking time: 5 minutes

Servings: 4 people

Ingredients:

- 1-ounce pork rinds, finely ground
- 2 medium avocados

Directions:

1. Split each avocado in half. Now have the pit removed. Peel the outer gently and then split the flesh into 1/4'-thick strips.

2. Put the pork rinds in a medium-sized pot and drop each slice of avocado onto your pork rinds to cover it fully. Put the pieces of avocado in the bucket of your air fryer.

3. Set the temperature and adjust the clock to about 350°F for around 5 minutes.

4. Instantly serve.

3. Flatbread

Preparation time: 5 minutes

Cooking time: 7 minutes

Servings: 2 people

Ingredients:

- 1-ounce full-fat cream cheese softened
- 1/4 cup blanched finely ground almond flour
- 1 cup shredded mozzarella cheese

Directions:

1. Meltdown some mozzarella in your microwave for about 30 seconds in a wide oven-safe container. Mix in some almond flour to make it smooth, and add some cream cheese to the mix. Proceed to blend until dough shapes, slowly kneading using wet hands if needed.

2. Split the dough into two parts and roll between two pieces of parchment paper to a thickness of about 1/4". Cut an extra piece of parchment paper to fit in the container of your air fryer.

3. Put a small piece of flatbread; try working in two batches if necessary, on your parchment paper and into the air fryer.

4. Set the temperature and adjust the clock to about 320 ° F for around 7 minutes.

5. Rotate the flatbread midway through the cooking process. Serve it hot.

4. Radish Chips

Preparation time: 10 minutes

Cooking time: 5 minutes

Servings: 4 people

Ingredients:

- 2 tablespoons coconut oil, melted
- 1/2 teaspoon garlic powder
- 1/4 teaspoon paprika
- 1/4 teaspoon onion powder
- 1 pound radishes
- 2 cups water

Directions:

1. Put the water in a medium-sized saucepan and bring the water to a boil.

2. Cut the upper part and bottom of each radish, then cut each radish thinly and evenly using a mandolin. For this

stage, you can use the cutting blade in your food processor.

3. For about 5 minutes or until transparent, put the radish pieces in hot water. To trap extra humidity, extract them from the boiling water and put them on a dry paper towel.

4. In a wide pot, combine the radish pieces and the rest of the ingredients until thoroughly covered in oil and seasoned. Put the radish chips in the basket of an air fryer.

5. Set the temperature and adjust the clock to about 320°F for around 5 minutes.

6. During the cooking process, rotate the basket at least two or three times. Serve it hot.

5. Coconut Flour Cheesy Garlic Biscuits

Preparation time: 10 minutes

Cooking time: 12 minutes

Servings: 4 people

Ingredients:

- 1 scallion, sliced
- 1/2 cup shredded sharp Cheddar cheese
- 1/4 cup unsalted butter, melted and divided
- 1 large egg
- 1/2 teaspoon garlic powder

- 1/2 teaspoon baking powder
- 1/3 cup coconut flour

Directions:

1. Combine the baking powder, coconut flour, and garlic powder in a wide dish.

2. Add half the melted butter, some cheddar cheese, egg, and the scallions and mix well. Pour the mixture into a rectangular 6-inch baking tray. Put it in the basket of your air fryer.

3. Set the temperature and adjust the clock to about 320 ° F for around a 12-minute timer.

4. Take out from the pan to enable it to cool thoroughly. Slice into four parts and add leftover melted butter on top of each piece.

6. Dinner Rolls

Preparation time: 10 minutes

Cooking time: 12 minutes

Servings: 6 people

Ingredients:

- 1 large egg
- 1/2 teaspoon baking powder
- 1/4 cup ground flaxseed
- 1 cup blanched finely ground almond flour
- 1-ounce full-fat cream cheese

- 1 cup shredded mozzarella cheese

Directions:

1. In a big oven-safe dish, put the cream cheese, mozzarella, and almond flour. Microwave for about 1 minute. Blend until smooth.

2. When thoroughly mixed and soft, add baking powder, flaxseed, and egg. Suppose the dough is too hard, microwave for an extra 15 seconds.

3. Split your dough into six portions and shape it into small balls. Put the balls into the bucket of your air fryer.

4. Set the temperature and adjust the clock to about 320 ° F for around a 12-minute timer.

5. Let the rolls cool fully before serving.

7. Cilantro Lime Roasted Cauliflower

Preparation time: 10 minutes

Cooking time: 7 minutes

Servings: 4 people

Ingredients:

- 2 tablespoons chopped cilantro
- 1 medium lime
- 1/2 teaspoon garlic powder
- 2 teaspoons chili powder
- 2 tablespoons coconut oil, melted
- 2 cups chopped cauliflower florets

Directions:

1. Toss your cauliflower with coconut oil in a big dish. Dust some garlic powder and chili powder. Put the prepared cauliflower in the bucket of your air fryer.

2. Set the temperature and adjust the clock to about 350°F for around 7 minutes.

3. At the sides, the cauliflower would be soft and starting to become golden. Put in the serving dish.

4. Slice the lime and squeeze the juice over your cauliflower. Garnish using cilantro.

8. Green Bean Casserole

Preparation time: 10 minutes

Cooking time: 15 minutes

Servings: 4 people

Ingredients:

- 1/2 ounce pork rinds, finely ground
- 1 pound fresh green beans, edges trimmed
- 1/4 teaspoon xanthan gum
- 1/2 cup chicken broth
- 1-ounce full-fat cream cheese
- 1/2 cup heavy whipping cream
- 1/2 cup chopped white mushrooms
- 1/4 cup diced yellow onion
- 4 tablespoons unsalted butter

Directions:

1. Melt some butter in a medium-sized skillet over medium flame. Sauté the mushrooms and onion for around 3-5 minutes before they become tender and fragrant.

2. Transfer the cream cheese, heavy whipped cream, and broth. Mix until thick. Bring it to a boil and decrease the flame to let it simmer. Sprinkle your xanthan into the pan and turn off the flame.

3. Cut the green beans into 2-inch pieces and put them in a circular 4-cup baking tray. Pour the combination of sauce over them and swirl until they are covered. Cover the dish with the rinds of ground pork. Place it in the bucket of your air fryer.

4. Set the temperature and adjust the clock to about 320°F for around 15 minutes.

5. When completely baked, the top will be golden brown, and green beans would be fork tender. Serve it hot.

9. Buffalo Cauliflower

Preparation time: 5 minutes

Cooking time: 5 minutes

Servings: 4 people

Ingredients:

- 1/4 cup buffalo sauce
- 1/2 (1-ounce) dry ranch seasoning packet

- 2 tablespoons salted butter, melted
- 4 cups cauliflower florets

Directions:

1. Toss the cauliflower with the butter and dry the ranch in a wide pot. Place it in the bucket of your air fryer.

2. Set the temperature and adjust the clock to about 400°F for around 5 minutes.

3. During frying, rotate the basket at least two to three times. Take out the cauliflower from the fryer basket when soft, and then toss in the buffalo sauce. Serve it hot.

10. Kale Chips

Preparation time: 5 minutes

Cooking time: 5 minutes

Servings: 4 people

Ingredients:

- 1/2 teaspoon salt
- 2 teaspoons avocado oil
- 4 cups stemmed kale

Directions:

1. Toss the kale in some avocado oil in a wide bowl and dust it with some salt. Put it in the bucket of your air fryer.

2. Set the temperature and adjust the clock to about 400°F for around 5 minutes.

3. Kale, when cooked completely, would be crisp. Instantly serve.

11. Roasted Garlic

Preparation time: 5 minutes

Cooking time: 20 minutes

Servings: 12 people

Ingredients:

- 2 teaspoons avocado oil
- 1 medium head garlic

Directions:

1. Remove the garlic from any remaining excess peel. However, keep the cloves protected. Slice 1/4 of the garlic head off, showing the tops of the cloves.

2. Add your avocado oil to it. In a small layer of aluminum foil, put the garlic head, tightly enclosing it. Put it in the bucket of your air fryer.

3. Set the temperature and adjust the clock to about 400 °F for around 20 minutes. Monitor it after about 15 minutes if the garlic head is a little shorter.

4. Garlic should be nicely browned when finished and very tender.

5. Cloves can pop out to eat and be scattered or sliced quickly. Up to 2 - 5 in an airtight jar store in the fridge. You can even freeze individual cloves on a baking tray,

and then put them together in a fridge-safe storage bag when frozen completely.

12.Zucchini Parmesan Chips

Preparation time: 10 minutes

Cooking time: 10 minutes

Servings: 4 people

Ingredients:

- 1/2 cup grated Parmesan cheese
- 1 large egg
- 1-ounce pork rinds
- 2 medium zucchini

Directions:

1. "Cut zucchini into thick slices of about 1/4 ". To extract excess water, put on a dry kitchen towel or two paper towels for around 30 minutes.
2. Put pork rinds and process until finely ground in the food processor. Dump into a medium-sized bowl and blend with parmesan.
3. In a shallow bowl, beat your egg.
4. Add the egg into pork rind mixture; soak zucchini pieces in it, covering as thoroughly as possible. Put each piece gently in a thin layer in the air fryer bucket, working as required in groups or individually.

5. Set the temperature and adjust the clock to about 320 degrees F for around 10 minutes.

6. Midway through the cooking process, turn your chips. Serve hot.

13. Crispy Brussels sprouts

Preparation time: 5 minutes

Cooking time: 10 minutes

Servings: 4 people

Ingredients:

- 1 tablespoon unsalted butter, melted
- 1 tablespoon coconut oil
- 1 pound Brussels sprouts

Directions:

1. Please remove all of the loose leaves from the Brussels sprouts and break them in half.

2. Sprinkle the sprouts with some coconut oil and placed them in the bowl of your air fryer.

3. Set the temperature and adjust the clock to about 400 ° F and for around10 minutes. Based on how they tend to cook, you might want to softly mix midway through the cooking period.

4. They should be soft with deeper caramelized spots when fully baked. Take out from the bucket of fryers and drizzle some melted butter. Serve instantly.

14. Cheesy Cauliflower Tots

Preparation time: 15 minutes

Cooking time: 12 minutes

Servings: 4 people

Ingredients:

- 1/8 teaspoon onion powder
- 1/4 teaspoon dried parsley
- 1/4 teaspoon garlic powder
- 1 large egg
- 1/2 cup grated Parmesan cheese
- 1 cup shredded mozzarella cheese
- 1 large head cauliflower

Directions:

1. Fill a big pot with 2 cups of water on the cooktop and put a steamer in the pot. Bring the water to a boil. Chop

the cauliflower into florets and put it on a steamer bowl. Close the pot with a lid.

2. Enable cauliflower to steam for around 7 minutes before they are tender fork. Take out your cauliflower from the steamer basket and put it in a cheesecloth or dry kitchen towel, and leave it to cool down. Squeeze over the sink and extract as much extra moisture as necessary. If not all the moisture is extracted, the mixture would be too fragile to shape into tots. Crush to a smooth consistency using a fork.

3. Add in some parmesan, mozzarella, parsley, garlic powder, egg, and onion powder and place the cauliflower in a big mixing dish. Stir when thoroughly mixed. The paste should be sticky but hard to shape.

4. Roll into tot form by taking 2 teaspoons of the mix. Repeat for the remaining mixture. Put in the bucket of your air fryer.

5. Set the temperature and Adjust the clock to about 320 ° F for around 12-minute.

6. Switch tots midway through the cooking period. When fully baked, cauliflower tots should be crispy. Serve hot.

15. Sausage-Stuffed Mushroom Caps

Preparation time: 10 minutes

Cooking time: 8 minutes

Servings: 2 people

Ingredients:

- 1 teaspoon minced fresh garlic
- 1/4 cup grated Parmesan cheese
- 2 tablespoons blanched finely ground almond flour
- 1/4 cup chopped onion
- 1/2 pound Italian sausage
- 6 large Portobello mushroom caps

Directions:

1. Using a spoon, voiding scrapings, to hollow out each mushroom shell.

2. Brown the sausage for approximately 10 minutes or until thoroughly baked, and no red exists in a small-sized skillet over medium flame. Drain and then add some reserved mushroom scrapings, parmesan, almond flour, onion, and garlic. Fold ingredients softly together and proceed to cook for an extra minute, and then remove from flame.

3. Pour the mixture uniformly into mushroom caps and put the caps in a circular 6-inch pot. Put the pan in the bucket of your air fryer.

4. Set the temperature and adjust the clock to about 375 °F for around 8 minutes.

5. The tops would be browned and fizzing when it is cooked completely. Serve it hot.

16. Garlic Herb Butter Roasted Radishes

Preparation time: 10 minutes

Cooking time: 10 minutes

Servings: 4 people

Ingredients:

- black pepper
- 1/4 teaspoon ground
- 1/4 teaspoon dried oregano
- 1/2 teaspoon dried parsley
- 1/2 teaspoon garlic powder
- 2 tablespoons unsalted butter, melted
- 1 pound radishes

Directions:

1. Remove the radish roots and split them into quarters.
2. Put seasonings and butter in a shallow dish. In the herb butter, turn the radishes and put them in your air-fryer basket.
3. Set the temperature and adjust the clock to about 350°F for around 10 minutes.
4. Simply throw the radishes in the air fryer basket midway through the cooking time. Keep cooking until the edges start to turn dark brown.

5. Serve it hot.

17. Loaded Roasted Broccoli

Preparation time: 10 minutes

Cooking time: 10 minutes

Servings: 3 people

Ingredients:

- 1 scallion, sliced on the bias
- 4 slices sugar-free bacon, cooked and crumbled
- 1/4 cup full-fat sour cream
- 1/2 cup shredded sharp Cheddar cheese
- 1 tablespoon coconut oil
- 3 cups fresh broccoli florets

Directions:

1. In the air fryer basket, put the broccoli and drizzle with some coconut oil.
2. Set the temperature and adjust the clock to about 350°F for around 10 minutes.
3. During frying, turn the basket at least two to three times to prevent burning.
4. Remove from the fryer as the broccoli continues to crisp at the ends. Garnish with some scallion slices and finish with sour cream, melted cheese, and crumbled bacon.

CHAPTER 4: Air Fryer Snack and Appetizer Recipes

1. Bacon-Wrapped Brie

Preparation time: 5 minutes

Cooking time: 10 minutes

Servings: 8 people

Ingredients:

- 1 (8-ounce) round Brie

- 4 slices sugar-free bacon

Directions:

1. To shape an X, position two bacon strips. Put the third bacon strip over the middle of the X sideways. Position vertically over the X a fourth slice of bacon. On top of your X, it could appear like an addition sign (+). Position the Brie in the middle of the bacon.

2. Tie the bacon from around Brie, using several toothpicks to hold it. To suit your air-fryer container, take a piece of parchment paper and put your bacon-wrapped Brie on it. Put it in the container of your air fryer.

3. Set the temperature and set the clock to about 400°F for around 10 minutes.

4. When there are only 3 minutes left on the clock, rotate Brie gently.

5. The bacon will be crispy when grilled, and the cheese will be smooth and melted. Cut into eight pieces to serve.

2. Crust less Meat Pizza

Preparation time: 5 minutes

Cooking time: 5 minutes

Servings: 1 people

Ingredients:

- 2 tablespoons low-carb, sugar-free pizza sauce for dipping
- 1 tablespoon grated or cutup Parmesan cheese

- 2 slices sugar-free bacon, cooked and crumbled
- 1/4 cup cooked ground sausage
- 7 slices pepperoni
- 1/2 cup shredded mozzarella cheese

Directions:

1. Line the bottom of a mozzarella 6' cake tray. Put on top of your cheese some sausage, pepperoni, and bacon and cover with parmesan. Put the pan in the bowl of your air fryer.

2. Set the temperature and set the clock to about 400°F for around 5 minutes.

3. Remove from the flame once the cheese is fizzing and lightly golden. Serve hot with some pizza sauce as dipping.

3. Garlic Cheese Bread

Preparation time: 10 minutes

Cooking time: 10 minutes

Servings: 2 people

Ingredients:

- 1/2 teaspoon garlic powder
- 1 large egg1 large egg
- 1/4 cup grated Parmesan cheese
- 1 cup shredded mozzarella cheese1 cup shredded mozzarella cheese

Directions:

1. In a big bowl, combine all the ingredients. To fit your air fryer bowl cut a piece of parchment paper. Add the blend onto the parchment paper to form a circle and put it in the air fryer basket.

2. Set the temperature and adjust the timer to about 350°F for around 10 minutes.

3. Serve it hot.

4. Mozzarella Pizza Crust

Preparation time: 5 minutes

Cooking time: 10 minutes

Servings: 1 people

Ingredients:

- 1 large egg white
- 1 tablespoon full-fat cream cheese
- 2 tablespoons blanched finely ground almond flour
- 1/2 cup shredded whole-milk mozzarella cheese

Directions:

1. In a small oven-safe bowl, put almond flour, mozzarella, and cream cheese. Microwave for about 30 seconds. Mix until the mixture becomes a softball. Add egg white and mix until fluffy, circular dough forms.

2. Shape into 6 round crust pizza.

3. To suit your air fryer container, take a piece of parchment paper and put each crust on the parchment paper. Place it in the basket of your air fryer.

4. Set the temperature and adjust the clock to about 350°F for around 10 minutes.

5. Switch sides after 5 minutes and put any preferred toppings on your crust at this stage. Keep cooking until lightly golden. Immediately serve.

5. Spicy Spinach Artichoke Dip

Preparation time: 10 minutes

Cooking time: 10 minutes

Servings: 6 people

Ingredients:

- 1 cup shredded pepper jack cheese
- 1/4 cup grated Parmesan cheese
- 1/2 teaspoon garlic powder
- 1/4 cup full-fat sour cream
- 1/4 cup full-fat mayonnaise
- 8 ounces full-fat cream cheese, softened
- 1/4 cup chopped pickled jalapeños
- 1 (14-ounce) can artichoke hearts, drained and chopped
- 10 ounces frozen spinach, drained and thawed

Directions:

1. In a 4-cup baking dish, combine all your ingredients. Put it in the basket of your air fryer.

2. Set the temperature and adjust the timer for around 10 minutes to about 320 °F.

3. When dark brown and sizzling, remove from flame. Serve it hot.

6. Mini Sweet Pepper Poppers

Preparation time: 18 minutes

Cooking time: 8 minutes

Servings: 4 people

Ingredients:

- 1/4 cup shredded pepper jack cheese
- 4 slices sugar-free bacon, cooked and crumbled
- 4 ounces full-fat cream cheese, softened

- 8 mini sweet peppers

Directions:

1. Cut the tops of your peppers and lengthwise cut each one in the quarter. Remove the seeds and cut the membranes with a tiny knife.

2. Toss the bacon, cream cheese, and pepper jack in a tiny bowl.

3. Put each sweet pepper with 3 tsp. of the mixture and push down smoothly. Put it in the air fryer basket.

4. Set the temperature and adjust the clock to about 400°F for around 8 minutes.

5. Serve it hot.

7. Bacon-Wrapped Onion Rings

Preparation time: 5 minutes

Cooking time: 10 minutes

Servings: 4 people

Ingredients:

- 8 slices sugar-free bacon
- 1 tablespoon sriracha
- 1 large onion, peeled

Directions:

1. Cut your onion into large 1/4-inch pieces. Sprinkle the sriracha on the pieces of your onion. Take two pieces of onion and cover the circles with bacon. Redo with the

rest of the onion and bacon. Put in the container of your air fryer.

2. Set the temperature and adjust the clock to about 350°F for around 10 minutes.

3. To rotate the onion rings midway through the frying period, use tongs. The bacon would be crispy once completely fried. Serve hot.

8. Mozzarella Sticks

Preparation time: 60 minutes

Cooking time: 10 minutes

Servings: 4 people

Ingredients:

- 2 big eggs
- 1 teaspoon dried parsley
- 1/2 ounce pork rinds, finely ground
- 1/2 cup of grated Parmesan or any other kind of cheese
- 6 (1-ounce) mozzarella string cheese sticks

Directions:

1. Put mozzarella sticks on a chopping board and slice in half. Freeze for about 45 minutes or till solid. Remove your frozen sticks after an hour if freezing overnight, then put them in a sealed zip-top plastic bag and put them back for potential usage in the freezer.

2. Mix the ground pork rinds, parmesan, and parsley in a wide dish.

3. Whisk the eggs together in a medium dish separately.

4. Soak a stick of frozen mozzarella into whisked eggs and then cover in Parmesan mixture. Repeat for the leftover sticks. Put the sticks of mozzarella in the basket of your air fryer.

5. Set the temperature to about 400 degrees F and adjust the clock for around 10 minutes or till it turns golden.

6. Serve it hot.

9. Pork Rind Tortillas

Preparation time: 10 minutes

Cooking time: 5 minutes

Servings: 4 people

Ingredients:

- 1 large egg
- 2 tablespoons full-fat cream cheese
- 3/4 cup shredded mozzarella cheese
- 1-ounce pork rinds

Directions:

1. Put pork rinds and pulses into the food processor pulse till finely ground.

2. Put mozzarella in a big oven-safe bowl. Cut the cream cheese into tiny bits and transfer them to the bowl.

Microwave for about 30 seconds or so; all cheeses are molten and can be combined into a ball quickly. To the cheese mixture, add some ground pork rinds and eggs.

3. Keep mixing until the combination forms a ball. If it cools too fast and the cheese hardens, microwave for another 10 seconds.

4. Divide the dough into four tiny balls. Put each dough ball among 2 pieces of parchment paper and roll into a 1/4" flat layer.

5. Put the tortilla chips in a thin layer in your air fryer basket, operating in groups if required.

6. Set the temperature and adjust the clock to about 400°F for around 5 minutes.

7. Tortillas, when thoroughly baked, would be crispy and solid.

8. Instantly serve.

10. Bacon Cheeseburger Dip

Preparation time: 20 minutes

Cooking time: 10 minutes

Servings: 6 people

Ingredients:

- 2 large pickle spears, chopped
- 6 slices sugar-free bacon, cooked and crumbled
- 1/2 pound cooked 80/20 ground beef

- 11/4 cups shredded medium Cheddar cheese, divided
- 1 tablespoon Worcestershire sauce
- 1 teaspoon garlic powder
- 1/4 cup chopped onion
- 1/4 cup full-fat sour cream
- 1/4 cup full-fat mayonnaise
- 8 ounces full-fat cream cheese

Directions:

1. Put the cream cheese in a big, oven-safe dish and microwave for about 45 seconds. Add the Worcestershire sauce, sour cream, mayonnaise, garlic powder, onion, and 1 cup of Cheddar and mix well. Add fried ground beef and your bacon to it. Sprinkle the leftover Cheddar on top of the mixture.

2. Put in a 6-inch bowl and dump into the basket of your air fryer.

3. Set the temperature and adjust the clock to about 400°F for around 10 minutes.

4. When the surface is golden brown and bubbling, dipping is cooked. Scatter pickles over the dish. Serve hot.

11.Pizza Rolls

Preparation time: 18 minutes

Cooking time: 10 minutes

Servings: 8 people

Ingredients:

- 2 tablespoons grated Parmesan cheese
- 1/2 teaspoon dried parsley
- 1/4 teaspoon garlic powder
- 2 tablespoons unsalted butter, melted
- 8 (1-ounce) mozzarella string cheese sticks, cut into 3 pieces each
- 72 slices pepperoni

- 2 large eggs
- 1/2 cup almond flour
- 2 cups shredded mozzarella cheese

Directions:

1. Put almond flour and mozzarella in a big oven-safe bowl. Microwave for a minute. Withdraw the bowl and blend until a ball of dough forms. If required, microwave for an extra 30 seconds.

2. Crack the eggs into your bowl and blend until the ball becomes soft dough. Wet your hands with some water and gently knead your dough.

3. Rip off two wide pieces of parchment paper and brush with nonstick cooking spray on each side. Put your dough ball between the 2 pieces, facing dough with coated sides. To roll dough to a thickness of 1/4', use a rolling pin.

4. To cut into 24 rectangles, use a cutter. Put three pepperoni pieces and 1 strip of stringed cheese on each one of your rectangle.

5. Fold the rectangle in two, lining the filling with cheese and pepperoni. Ends closed by squeeze or roll. To suit your air-fryer bowl, take a piece of parchment paper and put it in the basket. On the parchment paper, place the rolls.

6. Set the temperature and adjust the clock to about 350°F for around 10 minutes.

7. Open your fryer after 5 minutes and rotate the rolls of pizza. Resume the fryer and proceed to cook until the rolls of pizza are golden brown.

8. Put the garlic powder, butter, and parsley in a tiny bowl. Brush the mix over the rolls of fried pizza and scatter the pizza with parmesan. Serve it hot.

12. Bacon Jalapeño Cheese Bread

Preparation time: 10 minutes

Cooking time: 18 minutes

Servings: 4 people

Ingredients:

- 4 slices sugar-free bacon, cooked and chopped
- 2 large eggs
- 1/4 cup chopped pickled jalapeños
- 1/4 cup of grated Parmesan cheese
- 2 cups shredded mozzarella cheese

Directions:

1. In a wide bowl, combine all your ingredients. Cut a slice of parchment to match the basket of your air fryer.

2. With a touch of water, dampen both of your hands and spread the mix out into a disk. Depending on the fryer's

scale, you would need to split this into 2 small cheese bread.

3. Put the parchment paper and your cheese bread into the basket of the air fryer.

4. Set the temperature and adjust the clock to about 320°F for around 15 minutes.

5. Turn the bread gently once you have 5 minutes remaining.

6. The top would be golden brown when completely baked. Serve it hot.

13. Spicy Buffalo Chicken Dip

Preparation time: 10 minutes

Cooking time: 10 minutes

Servings: 4 people

Ingredients:

- 2 scallions, sliced on the bias
- 11/2 cups shredded medium Cheddar cheese, divided
- 1/3 cup chopped pickled jalapeños
- 1/3 cup full-fat ranch dressing
- 1/2 cup buffalo sauce
- 8 ounces full-fat cream cheese, softened
- 1 cup cooked, diced chicken breast

Directions:

1. Put the chicken in a spacious bowl. Add some ranch dressing, cream cheese, and buffalo sauce. Mix until the sauces are fully blended and completely soft. Fold the jalapeños along with 1 cup of Cheddar in it.

2. Transfer the mixture into a circular 4-cup baking dish and put the leftover Cheddar on top. Put the dish in your air-fryer basket.

3. Set the temperature and adjust the clock to about 350°F for around 10 minutes.

4. When cooked, it'll be brown at the top, and the dip will bubble. Serve it hot with some cut-up scallions on top.

14. Garlic Parmesan Chicken Wings

Preparation time: 4 minutes

Cooking time: 25 minutes

Servings: 4 people

Ingredients:

- 1/4 teaspoon dried parsley
- 1/3 cup grated Parmesan cheese
- 4 tablespoons unsalted butter, melted
- 1 tablespoon baking powder
- 1/2 teaspoon garlic powder
- 1 teaspoon pink Himalayan salt
- 2 pounds raw chicken wings

Directions:

1. Put the chicken wings, 1/2 teaspoon of garlic powder, salt, and baking powder in a wide bowl, then toss. Put the wings in the basket of your air fryer.

2. Set the temperature and adjust the clock to about 400°F for around 25 minutes.

3. During the cooking period, rotate the bowl two to three times to ensure even cooking.

4. Mix the parmesan, butter, and parsley in a shallow dish.

5. Please take out your wings from the fryer and put them in a big, clean dish. Over your wings, pour the butter mixture and toss until covered completely. Serve it hot.

15. Bacon-Wrapped Jalapeño Poppers

Preparation time: 16 minutes

Cooking time: 12 minutes

Servings: 5 people

Ingredients:

- 12 slices sugar-free bacon
- 1/4 teaspoon garlic powder
- 1/3 cup shredded medium Cheddar cheese
- 3 ounces full-fat cream cheese
- 6 jalapeños (about 4" long each)

Directions:

1. Slice off the tops of the jalapeños and cut lengthwise down the middle into two sections. Using a knife to gently detach the white membrane and seeds from the peppers.

2. Put the Cheddar, cream cheese, and garlic powder in a big, oven-proof dish. Stir in the microwave for about 30 seconds. Spoon the blend of cheese into your hollow jalapeño.

3. Place a bacon slice over each half of the jalapeño, totally covering the pepper. Place it in the basket of an air fryer.

4. Set the temperature and adjust the clock to about 400°F for around 12 minutes.

5. Flip the peppers halfway into the cooking period. Serve it hot.

16. Prosciutto-Wrapped Parmesan Asparagus

Preparation time: 10 minutes

Cooking time: 10 minutes

Servings: 4 people

Ingredients:

- 2 tablespoons salted butter, melted
- 1/3 cup grated Parmesan cheese
- 1/8 teaspoon red pepper flakes
- 2 teaspoons lemon juice
- 1 tablespoon coconut oil, melted
- 12 (0.5-ounce) slices prosciutto
- 1 pound asparagus

Directions:

1. Put an asparagus spear on top of a slice of prosciutto on a clean cutting board.

2. Drizzle with coconut oil and lemon juice. Sprinkle the asparagus with parmesan and red pepper flakes. Roll prosciutto across a spear of asparagus. Put it in the basket of your air fryer.

3. Set the temperature and adjust the clock to about 375 °F for around 10 minutes or so.

4. Dribble the asparagus roll with some butter before serving.

CHAPTER 5: Desserts

1. Mini Cheesecake

Preparation time: 10 minutes

Cooking time: 15-18 minutes

Servings: 2 people

Ingredients:

- 1/8 cup powdered erythritol
- 1/2 teaspoon vanilla extract
- 1 large egg
- 4 ounces full-fat cream cheese, softened
- 2 tablespoons granular erythritol
- 2 tablespoons salted butter
- 1/2 cup walnuts

Directions:

1. In a food mixer, put the butter, walnuts, and granular erythritol. Pulse until the items bind together to shape the dough.

2. Push the dough into a 4-inch spring form pan and put the pan in the bucket of your air fryer.

3. Set the temperature and adjust the clock to about 400°F for around 5 minutes.

4. Pick the crust when the timer dings, and let it cool.

5. Mix your cream cheese with the vanilla extract, egg, and powdered erythritol in a medium-sized bowl until creamy.

2. Pecan Brownies

Preparation time: 10 minutes

Cooking time: 20 minutes

Servings: 6 people

Ingredients:

- 1/4 cup low-carb, sugar-free chocolate chips
- 1/4 cup chopped pecans
- 1 large egg
- 1/4 cup unsalted butter, softened
- 1/2 teaspoon baking powder
- 2 tablespoons unsweetened cocoa powder
- 1/2 cup powdered erythritol
- 1/2 cup blanched finely ground almond flour

Directions:

1. Mix the almond flour, chocolate powder, erythritol, and baking powder in a big bowl. Stir in the egg and butter.
2. "Fold in the chocolate chips and pecans. Pour the mixture into a 6" circular baking tray. Place the pan in the bucket of your air fryer.
3. Set the temperature and adjust the clock to about 300°F for around 20 minutes.

4. A toothpick placed in the middle will fall out clean once completely fried. Please enable it to cool off entirely and firm up for about 20 minutes.

3. Cinnamon Sugar Pork Rinds

Preparation time: 5 minutes

Cooking time: 5 minutes

Servings: 2 people

Ingredients:

- 1/4 cup powdered erythritol
- 1/2 teaspoon ground cinnamon
- 2 tablespoons unsalted butter, melted
- 2 ounces pork rinds

Directions:

1. Toss the pork rinds and butter into a wide pan. Sprinkle some erythritol and cinnamon, and toss to cover uniformly.
2. Put the pork rinds into the bucket of your air fryer.
3. Set the temperature and adjust the clock to about 400°F for around 5 minutes.
4. Instantly serve.

4. Almond Butter Cookie Balls

Preparation time: 5 minutes

Cooking time: 10 minutes

Servings: 10 people

Ingredients:

- 1/2 teaspoon ground cinnamon
- 1/4 cup low-carb, sugar-free chocolate chips
- 1/4 cup shredded unsweetened coconut
- 1/4 cup powdered erythritol
- 1/4 cup low-carb protein powder
- 1 teaspoon vanilla extract
- 1 large egg
- 1 cup almond butter

Directions:

1. Mix the almond butter with the egg in a big pot. Add protein powder, vanilla, and erythritol to it.
2. Fold in the coconut, chocolate chips, and cinnamon. Roll into 1" spheres. Put the balls in a 6' circular baking tray and place them in the bucket of your air fryer.
3. Set the temperature and adjust the clock to about 10 minutes to around 320 °F.
4. Please enable it to cool fully. Up to 4 days in an airtight jar placed in the fridge.

Conclusion

These times, air frying is one of the most common cooking techniques and air fryers have become one of the chef's most impressive devices. In no time, air fryers can help you prepare nutritious and tasty meals! To prepare unique dishes for you and your family members, you do not need to be a master in the kitchen!

Everything you have to do is buy an air fryer and this wonderful cookbook for air fryers! Soon, you can make the greatest dishes ever and inspire those around you.

Cooked meals at home with you! Believe us! Get your hands on an air fryer and this handy set of recipes for air fryers and begin your new cooking experience! Have fun!